Wonder Zone Fact File

This booklet belongs to

.........E v e l y n.........

A Scientist at

....

© Scripture Union 2019

First published 2019

ISBN 978 1 78506 744 0

Scripture Union
Trinity House, Opal Court,
Opal Drive, Fox Milne,
Milton Keynes, MK15 0DF
email: info@scriptureunion.org.uk
www.scriptureunion.org.uk

All rights reserved. No part of this publication may be reproduced, stored in a retrieval system, or transmitted in any form or by any means, electronic, mechanical, photocopying, recording or otherwise, without the prior permission of Scripture Union.

The right of Alex Taylor to be identified as the author of this work has been asserted by him in accordance with the Copyright, Designs and Patents Act 1988.

Scripture quotations are from the Contemporary English Version published by HarperCollins*Publishers* © 1991, 1992, 1995 American Bible Society. Used by permission.

British Library Cataloguing-in-Publication Data

A catalogue record of this book is available from the British Library.

Printed and bound in India by Nutech Print - Services

Cover and internal design by kwgraphicdesign

Internal illustrations by Tim Charnick

Scripture Union is an international Christian charity working with churches in more than 130 countries. Thank you for purchasing this book. Any profits from this book support SU in England and Wales to bring the good news of Jesus Christ to children, young people and families and to enable them to meet God through the Bible and prayer.

Find out more about our work and how you can get involved at:

- www.scriptureunion.org.uk (England and Wales)
- www.suscotland.org.uk (Scotland)
- www.suni.co.uk (Northern Ireland)
- www.scriptureunion.org (USA)
- www.su.org.au (Australia)

Wonder Zone has been produced in collaboration with The Faraday Institute for Science and Religion. The Faraday Institute is an interdisciplinary research and communication enterprise linked to the University of Cambridge.

This project and publication were made possible through the support of a grant from the John Templeton Foundation. The opinions expressed in this publication are those of the author(s) and do not necessarily reflect the views of the John Templeton Foundation.

If these materials have inspired you to wonder, head to www.faradaykids.com for the chance to explore more about science, faith, and what God has made.

Welcome to your Fact File!

Here's where you can explore all the evidence from the Bible. You can test out what you discover at Wonder Zone and make up your own mind about Jesus!

The Bible is split into two sections (the Old Testament and the New Testament). These two testaments are split into books (the Old Testament has 39 books, the New Testament has 27). The books are split into chapters (the biggest book, Psalms, has 150 chapters!) and those chapters are split into verses (the longest chapter is Psalm 119 with 176 verses!). Sometimes you'll see a Bible verse written like this: Psalm 139:14. Here is how you tell which verse to read:

Psalm 139 : 14

Psalm means we need to look for the **Bible book of Psalms**. If you are not sure where this is, look for the contents page near the beginning of the Bible.

139 means we need to look for the big number 139; we call it **chapter 139**.

14 means we need to look for the little number 14; we call it **verse 14**.

Evidence of you!

At **Wonder Zone** you become a Scientist! Look at yourself in a mirror. What can you see? What colour is your hair? Your eyes? What shape is your nose?

Draw a picture of yourself here. (Or take a photo and stick it in.)

- What's your favourite part of being a scientist? Caring for the world? Studying animals? Finding out how things work?

Write or draw all about it below!

I EX EXPrcimentin

EXPERIMENT 1
The fun of discovery

Can you discover the **eight** differences in these pictures?

5

EXPERIMENT 1
What Solomon asks for

This is the story of Solomon and what he asked God for.

5 One night while Solomon was in Gibeon, the Lord God appeared to him in a dream and said, "Solomon, ask for anything you want, and I will give it to you."

6 Solomon answered:

My father David, your servant, was honest and did what you commanded. You were always loyal to him, and you gave him a son who is now king. **7** Lord God, I'm your servant, and you've made me king in my father's place. But I'm very young and know so little about being a leader. **8** And now I must rule your chosen people, even though there are too many of them to count.

1 Kings 3:5–8

Chat to the other Scientists in your Lab. Ask them these questions:

- What surprises you in this story so far?
- If you could have anything in the world, what would you choose?
- What do you think Solomon chose?

EXPERIMENT

9 Please make me wise and teach me the difference between right and wrong. Then I will know how to rule your people. If you don't, there is no way I could rule this great nation of yours.

10-11 God said:

Solomon, I'm pleased that you asked for this. You could have asked to live a long time or to be rich. Or you could have asked for your enemies to be destroyed. Instead, you asked for wisdom to make right decisions. **12** So I'll make you wiser than anyone who has ever lived or ever will live.

13 I'll also give you what you didn't ask for. You'll be rich and respected as long as you live, and you'll be greater than any other king. **14** If you obey me and follow my commands, as your father David did, I'll let you live a long time.

15 Solomon woke up and realised that God had spoken to him in the dream. He went back to Jerusalem and stood in front of the sacred chest, where he offered sacrifices to please the Lord and sacrifices to ask his blessing. Then Solomon gave a feast for his officials.

1 Kings 3:9–15

- Did you guess correctly? Did you guess that Solomon chose to be wise?

- What does "wise" mean? Ask your Researcher and Lab Technician what they think.

Write or draw your ideas here:

EXPERIMENT 1
What discovery do you want to make?

You'll uncover many things at **Wonder Zone**, but what discovery do you most want to make? Facts about the universe? How rainbows happen? How your heart works? Or something about God, the one who Solomon was friends with?

Write or draw it here!

Show your fellow Scientists what you decided!

Psst! You can do your own experiments at home – check out pages 30 and 31. Why not do one today?

EXPERIMENT 2
The wonders of the universe

Can you name some of the planets in our solar system? Match the names to the pictures.

URANUS
SATURN
EARTH
JUPITER
MARS

EXPERIMENT 2
Everything is awesome!

The world around us is amazing. The writer of this psalm knew that. He knew that God had made it all.

1 Our Lord and Ruler,
your name is wonderful
everywhere on earth!
You let your glory be seen
in the heavens above.

2 With praises from children
and from tiny infants,
you have built a fortress.
It makes your enemies silent,
and all who turn against you
are left speechless.

3 I often think of the heavens
your hands have made,
and of the moon and stars
you put in place.

4 Then I ask, "Why do you care
about us humans?
Why are you concerned
for us weaklings?"

EXPERIMENT 2

5 You made us a little lower
than you yourself,
and you have crowned us
with glory and honour.

6 You let us rule everything
your hands have made.
And you put all of it
under our power—

7 the sheep and the cattle,
and every wild animal,

8 the birds in the sky,
the fish in the sea,
and all ocean creatures.

9 Our Lord and Ruler,
your name is wonderful
everywhere on earth!

Psalm 8

- Which part of the psalm do you like best?

Can you make the psalm look awesome with pictures? Draw, doodle and write all around the page!

EXPERIMENT 2
What do you think?

You've read or listened to the poem from the Bible. But what do you think?

Write or draw your answers to these questions!

- How do you feel about God making the world and you?
- What do you want to say to God?

When you have finished, show the other Scientists in your Lab this page. Explain this page to them.

EXPERIMENT 3
The colours of the rainbow

Do you know what colours make up a rainbow?

Colour them in here!

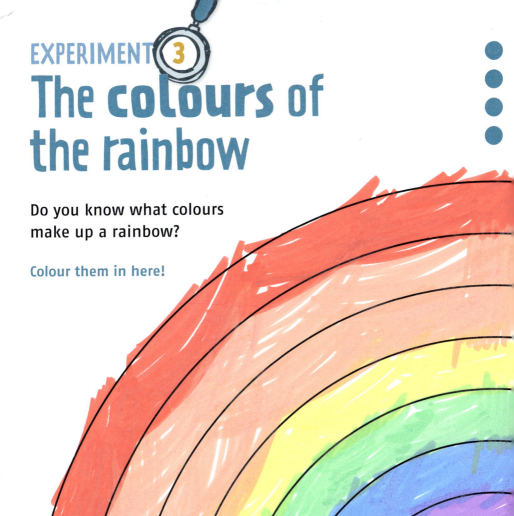

- What do you think of when you look at a rainbow? What about the other Scientists in your group?

Ask your Researchers and Lab Technicians what they think!

EXPERIMENT 3
Jesus brings some light!

¹ As Jesus walked along, he saw a man who had been blind since birth. ² Jesus' disciples asked, "Teacher, why was this man born blind? Was it because he or his parents sinned?"

³ "No, it wasn't!" Jesus answered. "But because of his blindness, you will see God work a miracle for him. ⁴ As long as it is day, we must do what the one who sent me wants me to do. When night comes, no one can work. ⁵ While I am in the world, I am the light for the world."

⁶ After Jesus said this, he spat on the ground. He made some mud and smeared it on the man's eyes. ⁷ Then he said, "Go and wash off the mud in Siloam Pool." The man went and washed in Siloam, which means "One Who Is Sent." When he had washed off the mud, he could see.

John 9:1–7

- How do you think the blind man felt when he wasn't blind?

Draw his face in here.

EXPERIMENT 3
What happened next?

Read what happened next (or get someone to read it to you!)

The day when Jesus healed the blind man was the Sabbath. This was God's special day. It was a day when everyone was meant to rest. The people in charge (they were called Pharisees) weren't happy. They thought Jesus was wrong to heal the man on God's special day.

They asked the blind man (remember, he was blind no longer!) what had happened. "Tell us the truth!" they said. "What he does is wrong!"

"I don't know if Jesus is wrong. All I know is that I used to be blind, and now I can see!" said the man.

The people in charge (the ones called Pharisees) were very angry. But the man knew that Jesus was special. He knew that Jesus was from God and that the people in charge were the ones who were wrong.

- What do you think of Jesus?

EXPERIMENT 3
What Jesus did

Jesus helped the man to see. The man's world was dark. But then it was full of light! Jesus changed the man's life! The people in charge were angry. The man was very happy!

- Do you want Jesus to do anything for you? What?

Write or draw it here.

Ask Jesus to help with what you have written or drawn.

EXPERIMENT 4
The creatures of the world

Go out into the garden or a bit of outside space.

- How many creatures can you see? Look in the grass, under rocks and in the sky!

Draw pictures of everything you see. If you know the name for it, write it next to your picture.

EXPERIMENT 4
God knows you!

God, who made the whole world, made you too. And he cares about you.

Read or listen to this psalm. How does it make you feel? Draw faces or stick in stickers to show how you feel!

¹ You have looked deep
into my heart, Lord,
and you know all about me.

² You know when I am resting
or when I am working,
and from heaven
you discover my thoughts.

³ You notice everything I do
and everywhere I go.

⁴ Before I even speak a word,
you know what I will say,

⁵ and with your powerful arm
you protect me
from every side.

⁶ I can't understand all of this!
Such wonderful knowledge
is far above me.

Psalm 139:1–6

EXPERIMENT 4

13 You are the one
who put me together
inside my mother's body,

14 and I praise you
because of the wonderful way
you created me.
Everything you do is marvellous!
Of this I have no doubt.

15 Nothing about me
is hidden from you!
I was secretly woven together
deep in the earth below,

16 but with your own eyes you saw
my body being formed.
Even before I was born,
you had written in your book
everything I would do.

17 Your thoughts are far beyond
my understanding,
much more than I
could ever imagine.

18 I try to count your thoughts,
but they outnumber the grains
of sand on the beach.
And when I awake,
I will find you nearby.

Psalm 139:13–18

EXPERIMENT 4
Did God make you?

This is our *Learn and remember* verse:

"I praise you because of the wonderful way you created me. Everything you do is marvellous! Of this I have no doubt."

Psalm 139:14

- Do you think God made you?
- How do you feel about that?

What questions do you want to ask God? Write or draw them here!

EXPERIMENT 5
The possibilities of robots

What choice would you make?

Read or listen to these questions. Then tell everyone what you would do!	How did you make your choice?
• Your mummy gives you some sweets. Do you share them with your friend? Or do you eat them all yourself?	
• You've broken a plate. (It was an accident.) Do you tell your daddy? Or do you not say anything?	
• You can have pizza or cheese sandwiches for lunch. What do you pick? Why?	
• Your grandma is taking you out! Where do you want to go with her?	
• There's a new child in your class at school. She looks sad. What do you do?	

EXPERIMENT 5
A father and his sons

Read or listen to this story. What do you think about what happens?

11 Jesus also told them another story:

Once a man had two sons. **12** The younger son said to his father, "Give me my share of the property." So the father divided his property between his two sons.

13 Not long after that, the younger son packed up everything he owned and left for a foreign country, where he wasted all his money in wild living. **14** He had spent everything, when a bad famine spread through that whole land. Soon he had nothing to eat.

15 He went to work for a man in that country, and the man sent him out to take care of his pigs. **16** He would have been glad to eat what the pigs were eating, but no one gave him a thing.

17 Finally, he came to his senses and said, "My father's workers have plenty to eat, and here I am, starving to death! **18** I will go to my father and say to him, 'Father, I have sinned against God in heaven and against you. **19** I am no longer good enough to be called your son. Treat me like one of your workers.'"

20 The younger son got up and started back to his father. But when he was still a long way off, his father saw him and felt sorry for him. He ran to his son and hugged and kissed him.

21 The son said, "Father, I have sinned against God in heaven and against you. I am no longer good enough to be called your son."

Luke 15:11–21

EXPERIMENT 5

22 But his father said to the servants, "Hurry and bring the best clothes and put them on him. Give him a ring for his finger and sandals for his feet. **23** Get the best calf and prepare it, so we can eat and celebrate. **24** This son of mine was dead, but has now come back to life. He was lost and has now been found." And they began to celebrate.

25 The older son had been out in the field. But when he came near the house, he heard the music and dancing. **26** So he called one of the servants over and asked, "What's going on here?"

27 The servant answered, "Your brother has come home safe and sound, and your father ordered us to kill the best calf." **28** The older brother got so angry that he would not even go into the house. His father came out and begged him to go in. **29** But he said to his father, "For years I have worked for you like a slave and have always obeyed you. But you have never even given me a little goat, so that I could give a dinner for my friends. **30** This other son of yours wasted your money on prostitutes. And now that he has come home, you ordered the best calf to be killed for a feast."

31 His father replied, "My son, you are always with me, and everything I have is yours. **32** But we should be glad and celebrate! Your brother was dead, but he is now alive. He was lost and has now been found."

Luke 15:22−32

EXPERIMENT 5
Draw your results

Use this space to draw pictures of the story. You could draw the younger son spending his money. Or looking sad with the pigs. You could draw the father waiting for his son to come home. Or the angry older brother.

When you have finished, show the other Scientists in your Lab. Tell them why you decided to draw your picture.

EXPERIMENT 5
What next?

You've discovered so many things at **Wonder Zone.** What do you want to discover next?

Circle some of these things, or write or draw your own ideas.

HOW GOD MADE ME

More about space

How a heart works

Who Jesus is

Learn and remember

Ants have escaped from the formicarium (that's the fancy name for an ant house). They have chewed out and run off with all the words of the *Learn and remember* verse.

Can you put them all back in the right place?

Discovering the God of creation

At **Wonder Zone,** you've been discovering so much about lots of different areas of science. And you've been exploring how faith and science go hand in hand!

Circle the picture that is closest to what you now think about God.

Chat to your Researcher about what you have circled. They would love to know and can help you, if that's what you want.

Try a new experiment

You heard lots about God at **Wonder Zone**. You might want to experiment with discovering more about him.

God loves everyone so much – he made this wonderful world and he made us too. He wants us to be his friend. He sent his Son, Jesus, to live with his people and show them the best way to live. (Jesus is light for the world, remember?)

If you want to know more, then chat to your Researcher or Lab Technician.

You might also want to say this prayer to God:

> Thank you, God, that you made such an amazing world. Thank you that we can live in this world.
>
> I want to know more about you and what you have done for me. Help me discover more about you!
>
> Amen.

Experiment away

Try these experiments at home!

Cress heads

You will need
- two eggs
- two egg cups
- felt-tip pens
- some cotton wool
- cress or mustard seeds
- water

This experiment will help you discover how important water is. It helps things to grow!

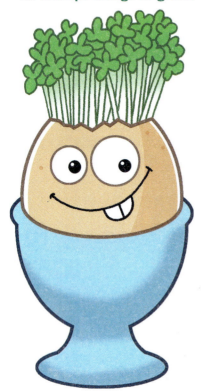

1. Ask an adult to carefully crack both eggs into a bowl. They should make the break two thirds of the way down the shell. Save the eggs themselves (you could cook those later!). Clean out the shells and put the bigger part of each one into an egg cup. Draw a face on each egg shell.

2. Put cotton wool in the bottom of each one and then sprinkle some seeds into each shell. Pour a little bit of water in one of the shells. Leave the other one dry.

3. Put the two egg cups on a sunny window ledge. Keep the cotton wool wet in one shell, but leave the other one dry.

4. After a few days, investigate what has happened. The seeds in the wet shell should have grown. The seeds in the dry one won't have grown at all.

What does that tell you about the water?

For more experiments, go to the Royal Institute website: www.rigb.org/families/experimental

Money cleaning

You will need
- some old 2p coins
- clean cloths
- toothpaste
- brown sauce
- cola
- two glasses

Your copper coins need to be quite dirty. The object of this experiment is to see what cleans coins the best!

1 Fill two glasses with cola and drop a coin into each one. Put these somewhere safe where they won't get knocked over.

2 Rub a coin with a clean cloth. How clean is it after you have rubbed it for a few moments?

3 Put some toothpaste on a cloth and wipe it over another coin. Rub the coin with the cloth for a few moments. How clean is the coin now? Compare it to the first coin.

4 Put some brown sauce on another cloth. Wipe this over another coin and rub it for a few moments. How clean is the coin now? Compare it to the other coins.

5 After an hour, take one of the coins out of the cola and wipe it dry. How clean is the coin now? Compare it to the others.

6 After a day, take the other coin out of the cola. Wipe it clean. How clean is the coin now? Compare it to the others.

What substance cleans coins the best?

31

My friends at Wonder Zone

You've met lots of new friends at **Wonder Zone.**

Use this space for messages, pictures and doodles from your Lab and others.

Don't forget your Researchers and Lab Technicians!